Science at Work in
FOOTBALL

By Richard Hantula

**Science and Curriculum
Consultant:**
Debra Voege, M.A.,
Science Curriculum
Resource Teacher

 Marshall Cavendish
Benchmark
New York

Published by Marshall Cavendish Benchmark
An imprint of Marshall Cavendish Corporation

Other Marshall Cavendish Offices:
Marshall Cavendish International (Asia) Private Limited, 1 New Industrial Road, Singapore 536196 •
Marshall Cavendish International (Thailand) Co Ltd. 253 Asoke, 12th Flr, Sukhumvit 21 Road, Klongtoey Nua, Wattana, Bangkok 10110, Thailand • Marshall Cavendish (Malaysia) Sdn Bhd, Times Subang, Lot 46, Subang Hi-Tech Industrial Park, Batu Tiga, 40000 Shah Alam, Selangor Darul Ehsan, Malaysia

Marshall Cavendish is a trademark of Times Publishing Limited

All websites were available and accurate when this book was sent to press.

Library of Congress Cataloging-in-Publication Data
Hantula, Richard.
        Science at work in football / Richard Hantula.
            p. cm. — (Sports science)
        Includes index.
        Summary: "Explains how the laws of science, especially physics,
are at work in the game of football"—Provided by publisher.
        ISBN 978-1-60870-589-4 (print) — ISBN 978-1-60870-672-3 (ebook)
    1. Football—Juvenile literature. 2. Physics—Juvenile literature.
    I. Title. II. Series.
    GV950.7.H36 2012
    796.332—dc22   2010052778

Developed for Marshall Cavendish Benchmark by RJF Publishing LLC (www.RJFpublishing.com)
Design: Westgraphix LLC/Tammy West
Photo Research: Edward A. Thomas

Cover: Wide receiver Andre Johnson catches a pass on the run.

The photographs in this book are used by permission and through the courtesy of:
Front Cover: Bob Levey/Getty Images.
AP Images: 4; Barry Gutierrez, 8; Ted S. Warren, 12; Kevin Terrell, 24; Charles Krupa, 26.
Getty Images: Eliot J. Schechter /Allsport, 14; Al Messerschmidt, 16; Andy Lyons, 22.
Newscom: Chad Ryan/Cal Sport Media, 6; x29/ZUMA Press, 7; Image of Sport, 10.

Printed in Malaysia (T)
135642

CONTENTS

Chapter One

Chapter Two

Chapter Three

Chapter Four

Words defined in the glossary are in
bold type the first time they appear
in the text.

CHAPTER ONE

Move That Ball!

Green Bay Packers quarterback Bart Starr (15) plunges across the
goal line to score the winning touchdown in the "Ice Bowl" in 1967.

Many football experts say the greatest game ever played took place in Green Bay, Wisconsin, on the last day of 1967. It pitted the Green Bay Packers against the Dallas Cowboys for the championship of the National Football League (NFL).

The game went down in history as the Ice Bowl. It was brutally cold in Green Bay that day. At game time the temperature stood at –13 degrees Fahrenheit (–25 degrees Celsius). There was a wind of 15 miles (24 kilometers) per hour. The field was frozen. Just holding on to the ball was hard. Each team had three fumbles. Both teams could not gain much yardage passing or rushing. Players found themselves slipping.

With only a dozen or so seconds left in the game, the Packers were losing, 17–14. But they were just 2 feet (0.6 meter) from the Cowboy goal line. Packer quarterback Bart Starr tried a simple sneak right into the Dallas defensive line. He made it. After kicking the extra point, Green Bay won, 21–17.

Push and Pull

Weather conditions in the Ice Bowl presented the Packers and Cowboys with a tough challenge. But they produced an unforgettable game by sticking to the basics of football. Football is really about two things: moving the ball and stopping the other team from moving the ball. The team with the ball may throw it or kick it or run with it. The other team may try to bat a pass down, block a kick, or tackle a ball carrier.

All these actions use some sort of push or pull. In other words, they use some sort of **force**. There is a branch of science that studies forces and how objects move and act on one another. It is known as **physics.** Scientists who specialize in physics are called physicists.

Oddball

Most balls are completely round. They are what scientists call **spheres.** Baseballs, basketballs, soccer balls, tennis balls, and volleyballs are all spheres. So are beach balls. The football is different. It is just roundish. It is like a sphere that has been pulled in two opposite directions. The name for such a shape is a prolate spheroid. Actually, since a football comes to a point at each end, it isn't a perfect prolate spheroid, either.

The football is probably descended from the soccer ball. (In fact, most of the world today still uses the name *football* for soccer.) For soccer, a round ball is perfect. It rolls easily along the ground. It bounces in a more or less predictable way.

But football is played differently from soccer, and that's why the ball has a different shape. In football, the ball isn't kicked very often. Usually, it is carried in a player's hands or thrown through the air. For these things, the football's shape is much better. A football is easier to hold on to than a soccer ball. It is also easier to throw. And it meets much less **resistance** from the air—at least, it does when a pointed end goes in front.

The football's shape makes it easier for players to hold. Shown here: quarterback Peyton Manning grips the ball as he gets ready to throw a pass.

Forces Galore

Physics can explain a lot about what goes on in a football game. Players produce some of the forces at work in football. They kick and throw the ball, for example. But these are not the only forces involved in the game. Another important force is **gravity**. This is a downward pull that Earth applies to the ball, the players, and everything else.

Still another key force is **friction**. This is a force that resists, or opposes, the motion of one object across the surface of another. Because of friction, a player can hold on to a ball. Friction also makes it possible to run without slipping. If a surface doesn't offer much friction— an icy field, for example—a person who tries to run on it may slip and fall.

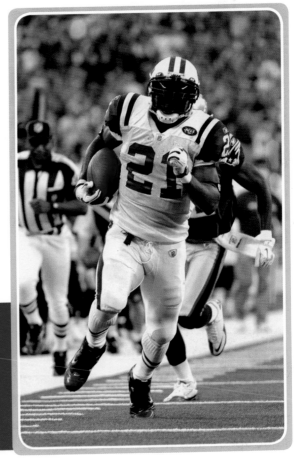

Friction helps a running back hold on to the ball and run without slipping. Shown here: LaDainian Tomlinson moves the ball downfield.

Friction has its limits. Shown here: the force of a tackle makes quarterback Tom Brady (12) lose his grip on the ball.

Forces caused by the air are also important in football. Wind, for example, can change the path of a ball that is passed or kicked. Even if there is no wind, the air creates a force that slows down a ball traveling through it. This force is called air resistance, or **drag**.

Newton's News

Many of the basic facts about forces and motion were explained by the English scientist Isaac Newton in the 1600s. Newton described how gravity works. He also described a few basic rules, or laws, of motion. The first of Newton's laws says that objects resist changes in their motion. A moving object will tend to keep moving at the same speed and in the same direction. This idea also applies

More than Speed

Some people use the word *velocity* to mean just "speed." But physicists use the word velocity in a special way. For them, it is the combination of an object's speed and direction.

By using velocity in this way, Newton's first law can be said very briefly: Unless a force acts, an object at rest will stay at rest, and a moving object will keep on moving at the same velocity.

to an object that is not moving at all. An object that is not moving has zero speed and is said to be at rest. It will tend to stay at rest. Physicists often use the word *inertia* to refer to an object's resistance to a change in its motion.

The first law also says that for an object's motion to change, a force has to act on the object. This means that an object at rest will start moving only if a force makes it do so. An object in motion will change its direction or speed only if some force acts on it.

The First Law Works

Newton's first law was at work when the Packers made the extra point after Bart Starr's Ice Bowl touchdown. The play started with the ball at rest. One of the Packers put it in motion by applying a force: he kicked the ball. Once the ball was kicked, it flew up between the goalposts. The first law of motion says that the ball would keep on going forever—unless some force kept it from doing so. A couple of forces did just that. As soon as the ball left the kicker's foot, air resistance started slowing it down and gravity started trying to pull it down to the ground.

PHYSICS FACT

First Law of Motion
If an object is at rest, it will stay at rest unless a force acts on it. If an object is moving, it will keep on moving in the same direction and at the same speed unless a force acts on it.

CHAPTER TWO

Running Hard and Quick

Running back Chris Johnson makes a 56-yard touchdown run in a 2010 NFL game.

The Tennessee Titans' running back Chris Johnson had a fine rookie season in the NFL. His second year, 2009, was phenomenal. He rushed for more than 2,000 yards. (1 yard is about 0.9 meter.) In the second game of the season, against the Houston Texans, the speedy running back put on a spectacular display. He totaled 197 yards in just 16 carries, including touchdown runs of 57 yards and 91 yards. He also racked up 87 yards as a receiver, 69 of which came on a touchdown pass. Johnson, of course, is an extremely good athlete. But part of his success lies in an ability to take full advantage of the laws of physics that govern football.

Changing Speed, Changing Direction

Each play in NFL football begins with the offensive team standing still in a set position. There's only one exception: one player in the backfield may be in motion, as long as he is not moving forward, toward the **line of scrimmage**. So when the ball is snapped to the quarterback, a running back such as Johnson either is at rest or, if in motion, is not getting any closer to the line. Either way, if he gets the ball, he has to be ready to change direction and speed up or slow down as the situation requires.

All of these changes in velocity—whether in speed or in direction, or both—are examples of what physicists call **acceleration**. People sometimes use *acceleration* to mean just "speeding up." But for physicists, the word is not limited in this way. In physics, acceleration means any change in velocity.

Second Law of Motion

For a change in velocity to happen, a force has to be used. Newton's first law of motion says so. Newton also described

Linemen at the line of scrimmage get ready to charge into each other.

a second law. It explains the relation between a force and the acceleration that the force produces in an object.

The second law of motion says that the acceleration depends partly on the size of the force. Suppose a strong force acts on an object. It will produce more acceleration than would a weaker force acting on the same object.

The second law also says that an object's **mass** affects how much acceleration the object receives from a force. The mass is simply the amount of matter in the object. A given force will produce more acceleration in an object with a small mass than in an object with a larger mass.

Slow Linemen

NFL backs and receivers usually run the fastest during a game. Partly this is because of the positions they play. It takes a little time to accelerate to a high speed. Runners like Chris Johnson start their runs in the backfield. A few seconds may pass before they meet up with a defender. They can use that time to pick up speed and look for an opening. If they find one, they can accelerate to top speed. Receivers typically have lots of room in front of them for acceleration. Offensive and defensive linemen, on the other hand, slam into each other as soon as the ball is snapped.

Also, NFL players on the line tend to be slow runners. They may be very strong, but they usually are not as fast as backs and receivers. That's because of Newton's second law. Linemen tend to have larger, more massive bodies. Their bodies have more inertia. Lineman need to use a lot more effort—a lot more force—to run fast.

PHYSICS FACT

Second Law of Motion

When a force acts on an object, the greater the force, the greater the acceleration it gives to the object. Also, if the same force is used on objects of different masses, the ones with less mass receive more acceleration.

Is Weight Mass?

Weight and mass are related, but they are not the same thing. An object's weight is a measurement of gravity's pull on the object. An object's mass is the amount of matter it contains. Gravity pulls more strongly on an object with a lot of mass than on an object with very little mass. So the object with a lot of mass weighs more. People say it is heavier.

But the force of gravity on Earth is different from the force of gravity on other worlds. The gravity on the planet Mars, for example, is weaker. On Earth, Chris Johnson weighs about 200 pounds (90 kilograms). On Mars, he would weigh only about 75 pounds (34 kilograms). His mass is the same on both planets. His weight is different.

Quickness Pays

Because of Newton's second law, it's hard for the NFL's massive linemen to accelerate, or change their velocity. This applies to all types of acceleration. Linemen generally cannot stop, start, or turn as quickly as most good running backs or receivers. Runners and receivers, with their smaller mass, have a built-in advantage.

They may find it harder to dodge defensive backs, who also tend to be fast and have a small mass.

Barry Sanders gets away from defenders in a 1998 NFL game.

But some runners and receivers can accelerate extremely quickly. They can make such fast changes in speed and direction—called juking—that they may fake even smaller defenders out of position. Legendary Detroit Lions running back Barry Sanders was a master at juking.

Third Law of Motion

Also important in running is the push a player applies to the ground with every step. This force helps make him accelerate. More exactly, it is one of a pair of forces that result in the acceleration. Another law of motion—the third law that Newton described—tells what is actually going on when the player accelerates.

Newton's third law says that forces come in pairs: If one object applies a force to another object, the second object applies an equal force to the first. In other words, for every force there is another force that is equal in strength but works in the opposite direction. This is sometimes said in a simpler way: For every action there is an equal but opposite reaction.

Newton's Third Law

Action

Reaction

The boy's throw pushes the big ball forward. The reaction force from the ball pushes him backward.

It is actually the reaction to the push by the player's foot that moves him forward. The player's foot pushes against the ground. But the ground is part of Earth, so the player is really pushing against Earth. Earth has a huge mass. Its mass is so enormous that the acceleration Earth gets from the player's push is very close to zero. But the player's mass is much smaller than Earth's. So the reaction force he receives from the ground is strong enough to move him forward.

PHYSICS FACT

Third Law of Motion
When one object applies a force to a second object, the second also applies an equal force to the first. In other words, for every action there is an equal and opposite reaction.

CHAPTER THREE
Air Attack

Quarterback Doug Flutie had an outstanding college career playing for Boston College.

Boston College quarterback Doug Flutie made a lot of headlines in fall 1984. He became the first passer to total more than 10,000 yards in a collegiate career. He also won the Heisman Trophy as collegiate football's most outstanding player. But today he is probably best remembered for a pass he threw at the end of a November game against the University of Miami.

Just six seconds were left on the clock, and Miami led, 45–41. Boston College had the ball around midfield. Flutie took the snap, scrambled back to his own 37-yard line, and heaved the ball as hard as he could. The wind was blowing in his face at 30 miles (48 kilometers) an hour, but the ball made it into the end zone and was caught for a touchdown. Boston College won, 47–45.

The ball traveled at least 63 yards (58 meters) in the air. It's hard for quarterbacks to make accurate throws over such long distances. Flutie's pass was a true Hail Mary. That's the name given to extremely long passes that are attempted when there's no time for anything else. The chances of a Hail Mary being caught are usually small. But Flutie's pass was caught. It became one of the most famous Hail Mary passes in history.

Gone with the Wind

It's easier for a skilled quarterback to keep short passes on target. But all passes, short or long—and all kicks—have one thing in common. They travel through the air. The air affects how the ball moves and what path it takes.

If there is a wind, the ball gets a push in the direction the wind is blowing. The effects of this force can be quite large when the wind is strong, especially when the ball goes a long distance or rises high in the air. But the effects can sometimes be hard to predict. When Flutie made his throw, the Miami defenders let a Boston College receiver get behind them in the end zone. They reportedly didn't think that Flutie could throw 60-plus yards against the wind. They were wrong.

Dealing with Drag

Even when there is no wind, the air pushes on the ball with a drag force. It keeps trying to slow the ball down. The strength of this force depends partly on the ball's speed. The faster the ball, the more resistance the air offers to the ball's flight.

Because of the football's shape, air resistance also depends on how the ball is thrown or kicked. One reason for this is that when an object pushes through air, its front part will meet more resistance if it is big than if it is small. So a football thrown with its fat midsection in front will meet a lot of drag. Passers instead try to throw the ball with one of its pointed

Thick and Thin

The strength of air resistance depends in part on the air's **density**—that is, how thick or thin it is. Thicker, or denser, air produces a bit more drag than does thinner, or less dense, air. This is because air is made up of particles of oxygen and other gases. In dense air, the particles are closer together. In thin air, the particles are farther apart. Many factors can affect the density of air.

One factor is the altitude of the playing field. Air at high altitudes is less dense than air at low altitudes. As a result, kicks tend to carry a few yards

farther at the Denver Broncos' home stadium, INVESCO Field, than at the Washington Redskins' FedExField. Denver lies about a mile (1.6 kilometers) above sea level. FedExField is located in Landover, Maryland, and is near sea level.

Temperature can also have a noticeable effect on air resistance. Hot air is less dense than cold air. For this reason, kicks in games played under a blazing sun at the Miami Dolphins' home field, Sun Life Stadium, tend to travel a few yards farther than kicks in wintry cold at Lambeau Field in Green Bay, Wisconsin.

Air Drag's Effect on a Punt

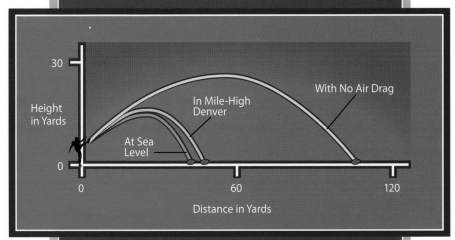

Air is denser—and causes more drag—at sea level than in Denver. If there were no air (and therefore no drag at all), a punt would go a lot farther.

ends in front. This gives the ball a streamlined appearance as it moves through the air. The ball causes less disturbance in the air, and so it meets less drag.

At the same time, passers try to make the ball spiral. When the ball spirals, it spins. It turns around an imaginary line, or **axis**, running through its center and its two ends. A good spiral can do a lot to lessen air resistance. It helps hold the pointed end of the ball in front, so the ball doesn't go end-over-end. A good spiral also helps keep the ball from wobbling too much. A serious wobble causes a big increase in air resistance.

Gravity's Effect

Like air resistance, gravity acts on a football flying through the air. Unlike air resistance, the force of gravity doesn't depend on the ball's speed. Gravity never stops pulling on the ball, and

Spiral Power

Every quarterback wants his passes to have a nice spiral. He wants to throw the ball so that it spins extremely fast around the axis running through its two pointed ends. It may turn hundreds of times a minute. Such a spin helps reduce air drag. It also helps keep the ball on course, lessening the effect of wind. All in all, spinning makes the ball's motion more stable. Physicists have a complicated name for the reason why this happens: conservation of **angular momentum**.

The basic idea in conservation of angular momentum is that a spinning object tends to keep on spinning. The object tends to resist forces that try to change the position of its axis. This is why a bike is easy to ride when its wheels are spinning rapidly. When the wheels are turning slowly or are not moving at all, the bike tends to tip over.

the strength of its pull on the ball is always the same (as long as the game is played on the surface of Earth).

Gravity's constant pull makes a long pass or a kick follow a path shaped something like a rainbow. At the moment the ball is thrown or kicked, it has a certain speed and moves in a certain direction. Usually the direction is somewhat upward. Gravity, however, pulls only straight down. It affects only the part of the ball's velocity that is in a straight up-and-down, or vertical, direction. If this vertical part of the ball's velocity is separated out, the rest of the ball's velocity is in a horizontal direction— parallel with the ground. The combination of the vertical and horizontal velocities is the ball's actual velocity.

Cannonball Physics

The same situation applies to any object that is thrown, or launched, into the air by some force. The path the object follows depends on that initial force but also on gravity and on forces caused by the air. Scientists call such an object a **projectile**. Cannonballs are projectiles. So are arrows.

As soon as a projectile is launched, gravity's pull starts reducing the vertical part of its velocity. The pull keeps working, and at some point reduces the projectile's upward speed to zero. The projectile then starts falling downward. Gravity's pull keeps trying to increase the projectile's downward speed, until the projectile hits the ground or is caught.

Meanwhile, the projectile keeps moving in a horizontal direction. Gravity causes no change in this horizontal velocity. If there were no air to slow down the projectile, the horizontal distance it covers after it reaches its high point would be the same as the horizontal distance it covers up to the high point. The projectile's path would be a type of curve, or arc, that scientists call a parabola. A projectile on Earth does meet air resistance, which slows its velocity, so its path is only similar to a parabola. The downward part of the path covers a shorter horizontal distance than the upward part.

Aiming High

Short bullet passes are usually thrown flat, or parallel with the ground. Their paths seem to curve hardly at all. This is because the ball's flight is so short. If the ball is not caught and continues to fly, gravity will pull it to the ground, making the curve easy to see.

Because a horizontal pass can't go very far before gravity pulls it to the ground, passers aim their long passes somewhat upward. This makes it possible for the ball to travel a greater horizontal distance before it lands. If a passer aims very high, however, most of the force of his throw will go to the ball's vertical velocity, and little will go to the horizontal velocity. In this case the ball will rise high up in the air, but it won't travel very far along the ground.

DREW BREES

The New Orleans Saints' Drew Brees has been one of the most successful quarterbacks in recent years. He is noted for a quick release of the ball and for an exceptionally accurate arm. The ESPN television show *Sport Science* once did a test to see whether he was as accurate at hitting a target as an Olympic archer. Brees threw a football at the target.

The archer shot arrows at the target from the same distance. Brees did much better than the archer. In fact, he hit the center circle on the target with all ten of his throws.

Born in 1979 in Texas, Brees went to college at Purdue University in Indiana. He played five seasons with the San Diego Chargers before landing in New Orleans. In the 2009 season, he completed 70.6 percent of his passes to set a new NFL record. He then led the Saints to victory in the 2010 Super Bowl. In the picture to the right, Brees gets set to pass during the Super Bowl.

Experts say that if there were no air, the best launch angle for the football to go as far as possible would be about 45 degrees. This direction is halfway between horizontal and straight up. Because of air drag, the actual best launch angle for maximum distance is often a little smaller than 45 degrees. Another reason for using a smaller angle is speed. A ball thrown at a smaller angle will reach the receiver slightly faster.

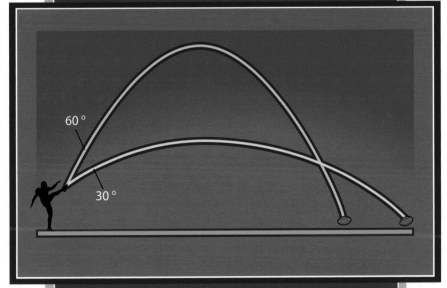

Launch Angle Affects Punt Distance

60°

30°

A high punt won't go as far as a punt kicked with the same force at a smaller launch angle.

Sometimes, however, a larger angle might be preferable. For example, a passer might throw the ball high if he believes his receivers need extra time to get into position. This higher throw creates longer hang time. The ball takes a little longer to get to its target.

Kickers also launch the ball at different angles, depending on the situation. They don't always try to kick the ball as far as they can.

Sometimes distance is less important than hang time. This is true especially in punting. The longer the hang time, the more time there is for the punter's team to get down field to cover the punt reception. So punts are sometimes made with launch angles as large as 60 degrees.

CHAPTER FOUR

Block and Tackle

Baltimore Ravens linebacker Ray Lewis leaves his feet as he tackles San Diego Chargers running back Darren Sproles during an NFL game on September 20, 2009.

One of the most unforgettable plays of the 2009 NFL season took place seconds from the end of a September game between the San Diego Chargers and the Baltimore Ravens. Baltimore had a five-point lead, but the Chargers were driving for a go-ahead touchdown. It was fourth down with 2 yards to go, and speedy San Diego running back Darren Sproles got the ball. He was still 5 yards behind the line of scrimmage when Baltimore linebacker Ray Lewis slashed into the San Diego backfield and smashed Sproles to the ground. Lewis's play saved the win for the Ravens.

Sproles is rather unusual for an NFL player. He weighs 190 pounds (86 kilograms) and stands only 5 feet 6 inches (1.68 meters) tall. Most players in the league are bigger. They have a larger mass. A big mass can help players deliver more powerful hits when blocking or tackling. It also helps them withstand hits that they receive. Lewis, for example, weighs 250 pounds (113 kilograms), and he is 6 feet 1 inch (1.85 meters) tall. And linemen are often much bigger than that! Sproles has been successful because he is very quick. But when a big man like Lewis runs straight into him, he most likely will end up on the ground.

Collision Force

Lewis and Sproles have different masses. But when Lewis ran into Sproles, each received the same force as the other. Newton's third law of motion requires this. Lewis acted on Sproles with a certain force. This caused Sproles to act on Lewis with a reaction force of the same strength.

Newton's second law of motion also applies. Because the two players differ in mass, the effects of these two forces were different. The player with the smaller mass—Sproles—received a greater change in velocity from the contact. Blocking is another example of Newton's second law at work. When one player blocks another, he pushes the second player. The bigger, or more massive, this second player is, the more force the blocker needs to use.

Amount of Motion

Two other useful physics ideas that can help explain what happens in blocking and tackling are **momentum** and **impulse**. A player's momentum is the amount of motion he has. It depends on both his mass and his velocity. For players with the same mass, those moving at a higher velocity have more momentum. For players moving at the same velocity, those who have more mass have more momentum.

Impulse is something that causes a change in momentum. It depends both on the amount of force applied

A defender trying to stop an offensive player has to apply force. How much force depends on how much momentum the offensive player has.

and on the time over which the force is applied. Suppose a defensive back needs to stop a big fullback rumbling down the field with the ball. The fullback is massive, so he has a lot of momentum. Or suppose the ball carrier is a speedy receiver. The receiver has less mass than the fullback but may be running so fast that he also has a lot of momentum.

In both cases, in order to make a tackle, the defensive back must apply a large impulse to overcome the ball carrier's momentum. One way to do this is to apply a big force quickly. But defensive backs tend to be smaller players. They may not be able to produce a big enough force. The other way to apply the necessary impulse is to apply a small force over a longer period of time. Often this is exactly what a small player does when tackling a larger one.

Energy Loss?

When objects are in motion, they have a form of **energy** called **kinetic energy**. So when a tackler chases a ball carrier, both players have kinetic energy. If the tackle is made, they both end up on the ground. Now neither player has any kinetic energy. What happened to it? This is an interesting question because one of the basic laws of nature is that energy cannot be created or destroyed. Physicists call this idea the law of conservation of energy.

PHYSICS FACT

Energy

Energy comes in different forms. Heat is a form of energy. So is light. Kinetic energy is another example of a form of energy. There's an important rule of physics called the law of conservation of energy: Energy cannot be destroyed. It can, however, be changed from one form to another.

The answer to the question of where the kinetic energy went lies in the fact that energy comes in different forms. Heat, light, and electricity are all forms of energy, for example. The different forms of energy all have the ability to do work. Although energy cannot be destroyed, it can be changed from one form to another.

When a tackle is made, the players' kinetic energy changes into other forms. Part of it turns into heat. If the tackle causes a fumble, a bit of the kinetic energy will be carried away with the ball. Some of the players' kinetic energy goes to shake up their bodies. This causes them pain. Sometimes it even causes injury. The greater the kinetic energy involved in a collision on the football field, the greater the possibility of injury.

Playing It Safe

Tackle football is a violent sport. Some of the most serious injuries that can happen are head injuries. They include the brain injury called a concussion. So wearing a helmet is a must.

Today's helmets have a hard shell, usually made of plastic. They have padding and special systems to help absorb and reduce the shock of a sudden impact. They also have face masks or face guards. Some have clear visors to protect the player's eyes.

Modern helmets can do a great deal to protect a player's head. Still, concussions can happen. Any player who is hit in the head and feels symptoms of a possible head injury—such as pain, dizziness, vision problems, or unusual behavior—should be checked by a doctor and follow the doctor's advice very carefully. A player should never ignore symptoms or hide them (perhaps to avoid missing playing time). Head injuries that are not properly treated can cause very serious problems.

To be on the safe side, the NFL in late 2009 adopted a new rule. It concerned players who are hit during a game or practice and develop certain head-injury symptoms. The players are not allowed to return to action until doctors—including an outside brain specialist—say they are OK.

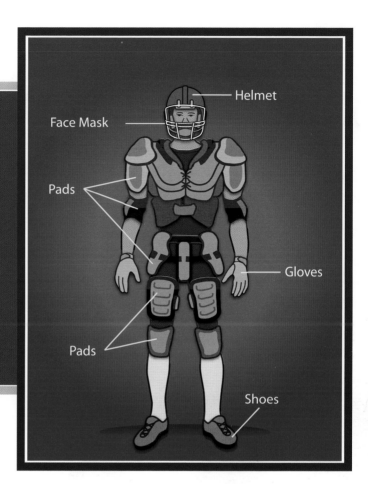

Helmet

Face Mask

Pads

Gloves

Pads

Shoes

Safety Gear

It's very important for football players to wear the right safety gear, including a helmet with a face mask, lots of padding, gloves to protect the hands, and the right kind of shoes to prevent slipping.

Good Gear

Luckily, improvements in helmets, pads, and other safety gear in recent years have helped hold down the risk of serious injury. Safety gear typically tries to reduce the shock of a collision with another player or with the ground. One way it does this is by keeping the energy of the impact from being concentrated on a single point on the body. By spreading the energy over a larger area, safety gear reduces the impact's effect at any individual point. Also, padding helps absorb the force. It weakens the impact by stretching the hit out over a slightly longer period of time.

acceleration: A change in velocity. As a measurement, it is the rate at which velocity changes.

angular momentum: A measure of an object's spinning motion.

axis: In a spinning ball, the imaginary line running through the ball's center around which the ball turns.

density: How close together the particles are that make up a gas. Air with particles that are close together is denser than air where there is more space between the particles.

drag: Air resistance; a force that slows an object moving through the air.

energy: In physics, the ability to do work.

force: Anything that causes a change in the velocity of an object, such as a push or a pull.

friction: A force resisting the movement of an object across a surface.

gravity: A force that pulls objects toward the center of Earth.

impulse: Something that changes the momentum of an object. As a measurement, it equals the force applied to the object multiplied by the time during which that force is applied.

inertia: The tendency of an object to resist being accelerated. A force has to be applied in order to put into motion an object that is at rest or to change the velocity of an object that is moving.

kinetic energy: The energy of a moving object.

line of scrimmage: An imaginary line running across a football field where the offensive and defensive teams line up at the beginning of a play.

mass: The amount of matter in an object.

momentum: A measure of an object's motion in a straight line. It equals the object's mass multiplied by its velocity. For spinning objects, there is a related idea called angular momentum.

physics: The branch of science dealing with matter and energy. Scientists who work in physics are called physicists. They study such things as moving objects.

projectile: An object that has been put into motion in the air by some force.

resistance: Opposition to the movement of an object.

sphere: An object that is completely round. Every point on its surface lies at the same distance from its center.

velocity: In physics, the speed and direction of a moving object. Some people use the word to mean simply "speed."

FIND OUT MORE

BOOKS

Biskup, Agnieszka. *Football: How It Works*. Mankato, MN: Capstone Press, 2010.

Gifford, Clive. *Football*. New York: Marshall Cavendish Benchmark, 2010.

Jacobs, Greg. *Everything Kids' Football Book, 2nd edition*. Avon, MA: Adams Media, 2010.

Silverstein, Alvin, Virginia Silverstein, and Laura Silverstein Nunn. *Forces and Motion*. Minneapolis, MN: Twenty-First Century Books, 2009.

Sohn, Emily. *A Crash Course in Forces and Motion with Max Axiom, Super Scientist*. Mankato, MN: Capstone Press, 2007.

WEBSITES

www.howstuffworks.com/physics-of-football.htm
Part of the Howstuffworks website, this webpage talks about some of the ways physics plays a key role in football.

www.nfl.com/rulebook
This National Football League webpage includes links to information about NFL rules and the basics of the game. The link called Record & Fact Book provides historical information.

http://physics.unl.edu/outreach/football.html
This site from the University of Nebraska contains short videos showing physics expert Timothy Gay explaining the scientific basis of football.

www.sportspectator.com/fancentral/football.html
This website has information about football rules, how the game is played, and its history.

INDEX

Page numbers in **bold** type are for photos, charts, and illustrations.

About the Author

Richard Hantula has written, edited, and translated books and articles on science and technology for more than three decades. He was the senior U.S. editor for the *Macmillan Encyclopedia of Science*.

19.95